To:

From:

Flowers appear on the earth;
the season of singing has come.

Song of Songs 2:12

Bouquets of Blessing
Copyright 2000 by ZondervanPublishingHouse
ISBN 0–310-97780-0

Requests for information should be addressed to:

ZondervanPublishingHouse
Grand Rapids, Michigan 49530
http://www.zondervan.com

Senior Editor: Gwen Ellis
Compiler: Marguerite LePley
Flower Arrangements: Patti Matthews
Designer: Steve Diggs and Friends
Photography: Photographic Concepts
Interior Design: Amy E. Langeler
Wedding Bouquet Design: Karla Anderson

Printed in China

00 01 02 03 / HK / 4 3 2 1

Bouquets

# of Blessing

Creating Special Bouquets
Using the Language of Flowers

Zondervan*Gifts*

We have a gift for inspiration™

Introduction

The bouquets in this book are not only delightful to look at, they send messages of encouragement, congratulations, concern, and caring to those you love. As early as Grecian and Roman times, flowers and greens have been assigned meanings. In the seventeenth century a French writer published a dictionary that formalized the "Language of Flowers."

In the Victorian era, a young woman's education was not considered complete until she had mastered the language of flowers. In the Victorian era, fragrant flowers were arranged into little nosegays called Tussie-Mussies. Ladies of distinction held them to their noses to cover the smells of primitive sanitation and infrequent bathing. Later, those same little bouquets became a way of sending messages. By combining certain flowers, a secret sentiment could be sent between friends or lovers.

Here the ancient idea of sending a message using flowers is combined with the Christian meanings for the flowers. In each section of this book you will find first a picture of the bouquet labeled with the occasion for which it is intended. The flowers in most of these bouquets are available all year either from your garden or from a florist. Those flowers not available all year have been indicated.

Next you will find simple instructions for constructing the bouquet, along with a list of supplies you will need. This page also has the meaning of the individual flowers and the sentiment the entire bouquet conveys. You can use either our sentiment or you can write your own on a card to attach to your bouquet. The following page of each section has Scriptures that speak to the meaning of the bouquet. The last page contains a lovely thought for your encouragement or to add to a card sent along with your personalized bouquet.

These bouquets are not difficult to construct and you need not limit yourself to just the flowers in the bouquet. If you cannot locate a certain flower, choose another from one of the other flower lists.

If you would like to send a special message to a friend or a family member that is unique and completely charming, read on and enjoy.

Table of Contents

God is Faithful

Creating the Bouquet

Get a large, clear vase. Begin filling it with stems of pink lilies. Next add pink gladiolas. The stems of both should be about twelve to fifteen inches long. Work stems of heather in around the lilies. Add white chrysanthemums throughout the bouquet.

Supplies
• Clear vase

Meaning of Flowers

Chrysanthemum, *white*—**Truth**

Gladiolus, *many colors*—**Strength of character, generosity**

Lily, *many colors*—**Majesty, resurrection**

Heather, *pink, purple*—**Protection from danger**

Thoughtful additions if available

Globe Amaranth—purpose, immortality, eternal love

Sweet Woodruff—eternal life, rejoicing

Meaning of Bouquet

May you be filled with confidence and hope in the strength and truth of God's love and majesty. May he guide and protect you; love and generously bless you; and give you the security of eternal life. He is worthy of our devotion and our trust.

Blessed is he whose help is the God
of Jacob, whose hope is in the Lord his
God, the Maker of heaven and earth, the sea,
and everything in them— the Lord,
who remains faithful forever.

Psalm 146:5—6

Those who know your name will trust in
you, for you, Lord, have never forsaken
those who seek you.

Psalm 9:10

"Because he loves me," says the Lord,
"I will rescue him; I will protect him,
for he acknowledges my name. He will call
upon me and I will answer him; I will
be with him in trouble, I will deliver him
and honor him. With long life will I
satisfy him and show him my salvation.

Psalm 91:14—16

Do not fear, for I am with you; do not be
dismayed, for I am your God. I will
strengthen you and help you; I will uphold
you with my righteous right hand.

Isaiah 41:10

His compassions never fail. They are new
every morning; great is your faithfulness.

Lamentations 3:22—23

For I am convinced that neither death nor
life, neither angels nor demons, neither
the present nor the future, nor any powers,
neither height nor depth, nor anything
else in all creation, will be able to separate us
from the love of God that is in Christ
Jesus our Lord.

Romans 8:38—39

For the word of the Lord is right and true;
he is faithful in all he does.

Psalm 33:4

The works of his hands are faithful and just;
all his precepts are trustworthy. They are
steadfast for ever and ever, done in faithfulness and uprightness. He provided
redemption for his people; he ordained his
covenant forever— holy and awesome is
his name.

Psalm 111:7—9

The lily bulb is buried deep within the dark, cold soil where it attracts no attention. It is dead to the rest of the world. But when the ground warms in the spring, a transformation begins. The bulb moves, the soil is pushed aside, and one day short green leaves push their way to the surface of the earth. The lily grows and puts forth a bud and then a pure white lily lifts its face to the sun. A man was buried deep within a dark, cold tomb. He was dead to the rest of the world. But as the third morning dawned, a transformation began. The earth shook, the stone before his tomb rolled aside, and the risen Jesus lifted his face to the Father. God is faithful in all things. In the same way that he is faithful to bring the lily from the ground in the spring, he was faithful to resurrect his Son so that we might have eternal life through him.

Molly Detweiler

Celebration

Creating the Bouquet

Sunflowers are so cheerful and showy that it doesn't take many to make someone's celebration very special. Gather eight blossoms into a hand bouquet and add sprigs of ivy. Tie with rafia and present to someone who is celebrating.

Supplies

• Rafia—available from a florist or a craft store.

Meaning of Flowers

Sunflower, *yellow*—**You are splendid**
Ivy, *green*—**fidelity, trust, ambition, tenacity**

Thoughtful additions if available

Morning Glory—the evanescent loveliness of life

Meaning of Bouquet

We rejoice with you as you celebrate this significant event in your life.

You have hung on with tenacity and your achievement is splendid!

The joy of the LORD is your strength.

Nehemiah 8:10

The cheerful heart has a continual feast.

Proverbs 15:15

Glorify the LORD with me; let us exalt his name together.

Psalm 34:3

Our mouths were filled with laughter, our tongues with songs of joy.

Psalm 126:2

Speak to one another with psalms, hymns and spiritual songs. Sing and make music in your heart to the Lord, always giving thanks to God the Father for everything.

Ephesians 5:19—20

God will bless you...in all the work of your hands, and your joy will be complete.

Deuteronomy 16:15

Shout for joy to the LORD, all the earth, burst into jubilant song with music.

Psalm 98:4

The LORD has done great things for us, and we are filled with joy.

Psalm 126:3

Joyful, joyful, we adore thee,

God of glory, Lord of love;

Hearts unfold like flowers before thee,

Opening to the sun above.

Melt the clouds of sin and sadness;

Drive the dark of doubt away;

Giver of immortal gladness,

Fill us with the light of day!

All thy works with joy surround thee,

Earth and heaven reflect thy rays,

Stars and angels sing around thee,

Center of unbroken praise;

Field and forest, vale and mountain,

Bloss'ming meadow, flashing sea,

Chanting bird and flowing fountain,

Call us to rejoice in thee.

Henry Van Dyke

Happy Birthday to You

Creating the Bouquet

*H*ere is a cheerful bouquet to celebrate someone's birth. There are two varieties of chrysanthemums shown in the bouquet—an open, white daisy-like variety, and a small, golden button variety. Cut them so the stems are about eight to twelve inches long. In your hand, gather the chrysanthemums, along with mini-carnation buds, pink asters, and pink and blue larkspur. Tie with a narrow, pink satin ribbon and a card.

Supplies
• Narrow pink satin ribbon
• Card

Meaning of Flowers

Chrysanthemum, *many colors*—**Optimism, cheerfulness, joy, mirth**

Mini Carnation Buds, *pink*— **Promise of good things to come, pure affection**

Delphinium, *blue, white*—**Well-being, sweetness, beauty**

Asters, *pink*—**Sentimental recollections**

Statice, *purple*—**Remembrance**

Bouvardia, *white, pink*—**Enthusiasm**

Stock—Lasting beauty

Evergreen—longevity

Alstromeria—Devotion, friendship

Meaning of Bouquet

On your birthday I wish you joy, well being, and long life. May you entrust your future to the Lord who will fill your life with sweetness and beauty. May you grow in wisdom, enjoy good health, and always remember with pleasure the years gone by.

You have been my hope, O sovereign LORD,
my confidence since my youth.

Psalm 71:5

Praise the LORD, O my soul, and forget not
all his benefits... who satisfies your
desires with good things so that your youth
is renewed like the eagle's.

Psalm 103:2,5

Since my youth, O God, you have taught
me, and to this day I declare your mar-
velous deeds.

Psalm 71:17

How much better to get wisdom than gold,
to choose understanding rather
than silver.

Proverbs 16:16

Sing and make music in your heart to the
Lord, always giving thanks to God the
Father for everything, in the name of our
Lord Jesus Christ.

Ephesians 5:19—20

Call unto me and I will answer you and tell
you great and unsearchable things you
do not know.

Jeremiah 33:3

May God himself, the God of peace, sanctify
you through and through. May your
whole spirit, soul and body be kept blame-
less at the coming of our Lord Jesus
Christ. The one who calls you is faithful and
he will do it.

1 Thessalonians 5:23—24

I have not stopped giving thanks for you,
remembering you in my prayers. I keep
asking that the God of our Lord Jesus Christ,
the glorious Father, may give you the
Spirit of wisdom and revelation, so that you
may know him better.

Ephesians 1:16—17

ife owes me nothing. Let the years
Bring clouds or azure, joy or tears;
Already a full cup I've quaffed; Already
wept and loved and laughed, And seen, in
ever endless ways, New beauties over-
whelm the days. Life owes me nought. No
pain that waits Can steal the wealth from
memory's gates; No aftermath of anguish
slow Can quench the soul fire's early glow.
I breathe, exulting, each new breath,
Embracing life, ignoring death. Life owes
me nothing. One clear morn Is boon
enough for being born; And be it ninety
years or ten, No need for me to question
when. While life is mine, I'll find it good,
And greet each hour with gratitude.

Author unknown

For a Wonderful Mother

Creating the Bouquet

Use two dozen mixed white and yellow Gerbera daisies. Cut some stems longer and some shorter. Place the tall flower in the back to create the look of this bouquet. Add statice and ivy and tie the green glass vase with a sheer purple ribbon.

Supplies

- Green vase
- One yard of sheer purple ribbon

Meaning of Flowers

Gerbera Daisies, *many colors***—Beauty**
Ivy, *green***—Fidelity, constancy, friendship**
Statice, *purple***—Remembrance, gratitude**

Meaning of Bouquet

You are a wonderful mother to me. You have a beautiful spirit and a beautiful character that are unequaled. Your constancy and friendship have always been a deep source of encouragement to me. I will forever remember and be grateful.

We were gentle among you, like a mother caring for her little children.

1 Thessalonians 2:7

He settles the barren woman in her home as a happy mother of children.

Psalm 113:9

Charm is deceptive, and beauty is fleeting; but a woman who fears the LORD is to be praised.

Proverbs 31:30

Even when I am old and gray, do not forsake me, O God, till I declare your power to the next generation, your might to all who are to come.

Psalm 71:18

We will not hide them from their children; we will tell the next generation the praiseworthy deeds of the LORD, his power, and the wonders he has done.

Psalm 78:4

One generation will commend your works to another; they will tell of your mighty acts. They will speak of the glorious splendor of your majesty, and I will meditate on your wonderful works. They will tell of the power of your awesome works, and I will proclaim your great deeds. They will celebrate your abundant goodness and joyfully sing of your righteousness.

Psalm 145:4—7

A Mother's Love

A mother's love is something that no
one can explain—
It is made of deep devotion and of sacri-
fice and pain.
It is endless and unselfish and enduring,
come what may,
For nothing can destroy it or take the
love away.
It is patient and forgiving when all others
are forsaking,
And it never fails or falters even though
the heart is breaking.
It believes beyond believing when the
world around condemns,
And it glows with all the beauty of the
rarest, brightest gems.

Helen Steiner Rice

Thank You

Creating the Bouquet

Gather a lot of perfect pansies from your garden and place them in a tiny silver vase. This whole bouquet is only six-inches tall and is the perfect thank you gift. (Spring, summer, early fall.)

Supplies
Supplies • Tiny Silver Vase • Pansies — can be obtained from your garden or from a nursery as plants.

Meaning of Flowers

Pansy, *many colors*—**Loving thoughts, you occupy my thoughts**

Thoughtful additions if available

Daisy Fleabane—thank you

Mint—welcome, hospitality, warmth of feelings, wisdom

Statice—remembrance, gratitude

Meaning of Bouquet

This bouquet comes with many thanks for all you are and for all you do. I think of you often and want to thank you for sharing with me out of the goodness of your heart!

Jesus said, "The good man brings good
things out of the good stored up in
his heart."

Luke 6:45

May the Lord make your love increase and
overflow for each other and for everyone
else, just as ours does for you.

1 Thessalonians 3:12

Each of us should please his neighbor for his
good, to build him up.

Romans 15:2

I thank my God every time I remember you.
In all my prayers for all of you I always
pray with joy.

Philippians 1:3

Give thanks to the LORD, for he is good; his
love endures forever.

Psalm 106:1

So then, just as you received Christ Jesus as
Lord, continue to live in him, rooted and
built up in him, strengthened in the faith as
you were taught, and overflowing with
thankfulness.

Colossians 2:6—7

This service that you perform is not only
supplying the needs of God's people but
is also overflowing in many expressions of
thanks to God.

2 Corinthians 9:9

ive thousand breathless dawns all
new;
Five thousand flowers fresh in dew;
Five thousand sunsets wrapped in gold;
One million snowflakes served ice cold;
Five quiet friends; one baby's love;
One white mad sea with clouds above;
One hundred music haunted dreams
Of moon drenched roads and hurrying
streams;
Of prophesying winds and trees;
Of silent stars and browsing bees;
One June night in a fragrant wood;
One heart that loved and understood.
I wondered when I waked at day,
How—how in God's name—I could pay!

Cortland W. Sayres

Have a Lovely Day

Creating the Bouquet

To duplicate our Have a Lovely Day bouquet, gather seven peach-colored roses in your hand. Begin tucking in short sprigs of delphinium and tiny bits of mint. Still holding the bouquet in your hand, surround it with lemon leaves. These tend to have a mind of their own and turn at odd angles. To eliminate this problem, you may want to wire a single leaf by breaking the leaf off the stem and floral taping it to a wire stem. You will then be able to twist and turn the leaf any way you like.

When you have gathered the entire bouquet and are pleased with the results, floral tape the stem together for about two or three inches. Then trim the stems at the bottom of the bouquet so that they are even.

> **Supplies**
>
> • Florist wire — available in different thicknesses from a craft store.
>
> • Floral tape — a stretchy tape available from a craft store.

Meaning of Flowers

Delphinium, *blue purple, white*—**Well-being, sweetness, return of a friend is desired**

Stock, *many colors*—**Promptness, lasting beauty**

Rose, *peach*—**Let's get together**

Mint, *green*—**Welcome, hospitality, warmth of feelings, wisdom**

Lemon Leaf, *green*—**Zest, fidelity, discretion**

Thoughtful additions if available

Clematis—mental beauty, ingenuity

Sorrel—joy, parental affection

Angelica Leaf—inspirations, soaring thoughts

Lavender—devotion, success, tranquility (green part available all year, flowers in summer)

Meaning of Bouquet

This bouquet brings the hopes that your day is filled with sweetness, that your heart is content and singing with joy to the Lord. May your work be done with zest and your friends bring you happiness.

He wakens me morning by morning,
 wakens my ear to listen like one
being taught.
 Isaiah 50:4

Taste and see that the LORD is good;
 blessed is the man who takes
refuge in him.
 Psalm 34:8

By day the LORD directs his love,
 at night his song is with me—
a prayer to the God of my life.
 Psalm 42:8

Sing to God, sing praise to his name,
 extol him who rides on the clouds—
his name is the LORD—and rejoice
 before him.
 Psalm 68:4

Whatever is true, whatever is noble,
 whatever is right, whatever is pure,
whatever is lovely, whatever is admirable—
 if anything is excellent or praiseworthy—think about such things.
 Philippians 4:8

Godliness with contentment is great gain.
 1 Timothy 6:6

But may the righteous be glad and rejoice
 before God; may they be happy and
joyful.
 Psalm 68:3

A happy heart makes the face cheerful,
 but heartache crushes the spirit.
 Proverbs 15:13

The little cares that fretted me,
I lost them yesterday
Among the fields above the sea,
Among the winds at play;
Among the lowing of the herds,
The rustling of the trees,
Among the singing of the birds,
The humming of the bees.
The foolish fears of what may happen,
I cast them all away
Among the clover scented grass,
Among the new mown hay;
Among the husking of the corn
Where drowsy poppies nod,
Where ill thoughts die and good are born
Out in the fields with God.

Elizabeth Barrett Browning

Congratulations on Your Engagement

Creating the Bouquet

$\mathcal{U}$se a white or a clear vase. Insert about two dozen red roses, stems cut to the same length. Tuck bouvardia between the roses and add leather fern around the outside. Add a white satin ribbon and a costume jewelry engagement ring. (The one shown here is real.)

Supplies
• White or clear vase
• White satin ribbon
• Costume jewelry diamond ring

Meaning of Flowers

Rose, *red*—**I love you, desire, passion, harmony, joy, charm, beauty**
Bouvardia, *white*—**I love you enthusiastically**
Fern, *green*—**fascination, sincerity**

Thoughtful additions if available
Phlox—our souls are united, proposal of love, sweet dreams
Lily of the Valley—sweetness, return of happiness, purity, delicacy
Honeysuckle—bonds of love, generous and devoted affection

Meaning of Bouquet

This bouquet brings wishes of great joy on the occasion of your engagement. May you find growing happiness in the sincere bonds of love. God has prepared so many blessings for you!

Where you go I will go, and where you stay

    I will stay. Your people will be my people

and your God my God.

              Ruth 1:16

Be at rest once more, O my soul, for the

    LORD has been good to you.

              Psalm 116:7

Arise, my darling, my beautiful one, and

    come with me. See! The winter is past;

the rains are over and gone. Flowers appear

    on the earth; the season of singing has

come.

             Song of Songs 2:10—12

Love one another deeply, from the heart.

             1 Peter 1:22

Love is patient, love is kind. It does not

    envy, it does not boast, it is not proud. It

    is not

rude, it is not self-seeking, it is not easily

angered, it keeps no record of wrongs.

Love does not delight in evil but rejoices

    with the truth. It always protects, always

trusts, always hopes, always perseveres.

           1 Corinthians 13:4—7

Jesus said, "Love one another. As I have

    loved you, so you must love one another.

By this all men will know that you are my

    disciples, if you love one another."

           John 13:34—35

There are three things that are too amazing

    for me, four that I do not understand:

The way of an eagle in the sky, the way of a

    snake on a rock, the way of a ship on the

high seas, and the way of a man with a

    maiden.

           Proverbs 30:18—19

My love is like a red, red rose,
That's newly sprung in June:
My love is like a melody,
That's sweetly played in tune.

As fair art thou, my bonny lass,
So deep in love am I;
And I will love thee still, my Dear,
Till all the seas go dry.

Till all the seas go dry, my Dear,
And the rocks melt with the sun;
And I will love thee still, my Dear,
While the sands of life shall run.

Robert Burns

Congratulations

Creating the Bouquet

Fill a clear glass cylinder with lots of gold roses. About two dozen makes this stunning display.

Supplies
• Clear glass vase

Meaning of Flowers

Rose, *gold-colored*—**Absolute achievement**

Thoughtful additions if available
Magnolia Leaf—perseverance, sweetness, beauty
Heather—admiration, dreams accomplished
Daffodil—regard, respect

Meaning of Bouquet

The Lord has done great things for you. Congratulations on your wonderful achievement!

I will tell of the kindnesses of the Lord, the
deeds for which he is to be praised,
According to all the Lord has done for us.
Isaiah 63:7

Because you are my help, I sing in the
shadow of your wings. My soul clings
to you; your right hand upholds me.
Psalm 63:7—8

"Not by might nor by power, but by my
spirit," says the Lord Almighty.
Zechariah 4:6

Let us not become weary in doing good, for
at the proper time we will reap a harvest
if we do not give up.
Galatians 6:9

When God gives any man wealth and pos-
sessions, and enables him to enjoy them,
to accept his lot and be happy in his work—
this is a gift of God.
Ecclesiastes 5:19

Those who have trusted in God may be
careful to devote themselves to doing
what is good. These things are excellent and
profitable for everyone.
Titus 3:8

till upward be thine onward course;
For this I pray today;
Still upward as the years go by.
And seasons pass away
Still upward in this coming year,
Thy path is all untried;
Still upward may'st thou journey on,
Close by thy Savior's side.
Still upward e'en though sorrow come,
And trials crush thine heart;
Still upward may they draw thy soul,
With Christ to walk apart.
Still upward till the day shall break,
And shadows all have flown;
Still upward till in Heaven you wake,
And stand before the throne.

Happy Anniversary

Creating the Bouquet

Lay one to two-dozen lavender roses on a piece of cellophane on a table. Arrange the roses so they cascade. Lay pink tulips on top to just circle the roses. Tuck in lots of Baby's Breath. Tie a satin or sheer ribbon around all the flower stems and the cellophane.

> Supplies
>
> • Cellophane — from a craft store or flower shop.
>
> • Ribbon — from craft, fabric, or floral shops.

Meaning of Flowers

Rose, *lavender*—**Rarity, dignity**

Tulip, *many colors*—**The perfect lover, happy years, memory, charity**

Baby's Breath, *white*—**Pure heart**

Thoughtful additions if available

Stock—lasting beauty   **Aster**—sentimental recollections

Rosemary—remembrance, fidelity, devotion; "your presence revives me," wisdom, strong memory

Leather Fern—sincerity, fascination

Meaning of Bouquet

Happy Anniversary! As you remember your years together, may you be filled with thanksgiving to God and increased devotion to one another. Your love is a rare and beautiful example of eternal love. May all of your hopes turn to memories, and may all of your memories be sweet!

Fear the LORD and serve him faithfully with
all your heart; consider what great things
he has done for you.

1 Samuel 12:24

Blessed are all who fear the LORD, who walk
in his ways. You will eat the fruit of your
labor; blessings and prosperity will be yours.
Your wife will be like a fruitful vine within your house; Your sons will be like olive
shoots around your table.

Psalm 128:1—3

A wife of noble character is her husband's
crown.

Proverbs 12:4

Say to him: 'Long life to you! Good health
to you and your household! And good
health to all that is yours!'

1 Samuel 25:6

For this reason a man will leave his father
and mother and be united to his wife,
and they will become one flesh.

Genesis 2:24

Remember the wonders he has done, his
miracles, and the judgments he
pronounced.

Psalm 105:5

I remember the days of long ago; I meditate
on all your works and consider what
your hands have done.

Psalm 143:5

row old along with me!
The best is yet to be,
The last of life, for which the first
  was made:
Our times are in His hand
Who saith, "A whole I planned,
Youth shows but half; trust God:
See all nor be afraid!"

Robert Browning

I'm Grateful for Your Friendship

Creating the Bouquet

Choose a basket with a plastic liner. Visit a garden nursery and select potted daffodils and white hyacinths that are in bloom. Remove them from their pots and tuck into the back of the basket. Get some sweet alyssum and Johnny jump-ups (violas).

Remove them from their pots and tuck into the basket in the front, putting the lowest flowers in the front. Get a pot or two of mint and tuck into the bouquet as well. These plants can be transplanted to your friend's garden to bloom all summer.

Supplies
• Basket with plastic lining
• Potted plants

Meaning of Flowers

Sweet Alyssum, *white or purple*—**Worth beyond beauty**
Daffodil, *yellow*—**Regard, respect**
Heart's Ease/Johnny Jump-up, *purple, blue*—**Happy thoughts**
Hyacinth, *white*—**I pray for you**
Mint, *green*—**Welcome, hospitality, warmth of feelings, wisdom**

Thoughtful additions if available
Elderberry flowers—sympathy, kindness   **Buttercup**—rich in charms, cheerfulness
Lemon Leaf, *green*—zest, fidelity, discretion

Meaning of Bouquet

My friend, you have a worth that is far beyond beauty. Your cheerful heart blesses me. I love the warmth of your hospitality and your gentle and discreet words. I am thankful for you!

A cheerful heart is good medicine.

> Proverbs 17:22

The wise in heart are called discerning—
Understanding is a fountain of life to
those who have it.

> Proverbs 16:21—22

Perfume and incense bring joy to the heart,
and the pleasantness of one's friend
springs from his earnest council.

> Proverbs 27:9

Jesus said, "Out of the overflow of the heart
the mouth speaks."

> Matthew 12:34

If one falls down, his friend can help
him up.

> Ecclesiastes 4:10

Dear friend, I pray that you may enjoy good
health and that all may go well with you,
even as your soul is getting along well.

> 3 John 2

May the grace of the Lord Jesus Christ, and
the love of God, and the fellowship of
the Holy Spirit be with you all.

> 2 Corinthians 13:14

If we walk in the light, as he is in the light,
we have fellowship with one another, and
the blood of Jesus, his Son, purifies us from
all sin.

> 1 John 1:7

y favorite early spring flowers are Johnny jump-ups. They have sweet smiling faces, each with its own personality. They remind me of some wonderful jump-up friends in my life—people who have come into my life over the years at just the exact time I needed to see a friendly, smiling face. Each morning, the sweet, smiling faces of the small flowers look up at me as they settle their roots into the earth. I smile back as I see in them the faces of my "jump-up" friends.

Peggy Benson

God Bless You in Your New Home

Creating the Bouquet

Find a stunning vase. This one is a hammered metal cone with a loop for hanging on the door. Trim the stems of one-dozen pink roses and place them in the vase in a nice round shape. Add lots of purple statice. Tuck in tall stems of delphinium and some boxwood pieces. Then add light, airy sea statice to fill in the bouquet. This bouquet will air dry so that the recipient can keep it indefinitely.

Supplies

• Hammered-metal cone vase

Meaning of Flowers

Roses, *pink*—**Grace and beauty**

Statice, *purple, blue*—**Never-ceasing, gratitude**

Sea Statice, *light lavender*—**Remembrance**

Delphinium, *blue*—**Well-being, sweetness**

Boxwood, *green*—**Hard work**

Thoughtful additions if available

Oak—hospitality

Alstroemeria—friendship, devotion, pleasantries

Mint—welcome, hospitality, warmth of feelings

Sage—domestic virtue

Queen Anne's Lace—haven, home, comfort

Meaning of Bouquet

God bless you in your new home! You have worked hard to obtain it. May you live with never-ending gratitude to the One who has helped you. May your home be filled with grace and beauty, well being and sweetness. May it always be a haven of comfort and rest to your family; a place of warm welcome to friends and strangers.

Unless the LORD builds the house, its
builders labor in vain.

Psalm 127:1

The wise woman builds up her house.

Proverbs 14:1

Grace and peace to you from him who is,
and who was.

Revelation 1:4

May there be peace within your walls, And
security within your citadels.

Psalm 122:7

My people will live in peaceful dwelling
places, in secure homes, in undisturbed
places of rest.

Isaiah 32:18

Share with God's people who are in need.
Practice hospitality.

Romans 12:13

Mercy, peace and love be yours in
abundance.

Jude 1:2

I will lie down and sleep in peace, for you
alone, O LORD, make me dwell in safety.

Psalm 4:8

*H*ail, guest! We ask not what
thou art; If friend, we greet thee,
hand and heart; If stranger, such no
longer be; If foe, our love will con-
quer thee.

Welcome over the door of an old inn

Oh, love this house, and make of it a
home—A cherished, hallowed place.
Root roses at its base, and freely
paint The glow of welcome on its
smiling face! For after friends are
gone, and children marry, And you
are left alone, The house you love
will clasp you to its heart, Within its
arms of lumber and of stone.

Rosa Zagnoni Marinoni

God Bless You

Creating The Bouquet

This showy bouquet is not as difficult to create as it looks. Use a terracotta vase in green or gold. Trim yellow gladiolas so they are about three times the height of the container. Fresh gladiolas are mostly buds at the tips, but they will bloom out in a few days. Add yellow alstroemeria.

Since alstroemeria is readily available and is inexpensive, use lots of it to give fullness to the bouquet. Add plenty of yellow solidaster (sometimes called goldenrod) and white Queen Anne's lace. Finish the bouquet by tucking in galax leaves.

> Supplies
>
> • Terracotta vase
>
> • Queen Anne's lace — grows wild, but your florist has it too.

Meaning of Flowers

Gladiolus, *yellow*—**Strength of character, generosity**

Alstroemeria, *gold, yellow*—**Devotion, friendship, pleasantries**

Queen Anne's Lace, *white*—**Protection, haven, comfort, home**

Goldenrod or Solidaster, *yellow*—**Encouragement, blessings**

Galax Leaves, *green*—**Friendship, encouragement**

Thoughtful additions if available

Blue Salvia—wisdom, I think of you

Salad Burnet—a merry heart, joy

Viola/Johnny jump-up—happy thoughts

Meaning of Bouquet

May God bless you with the fruits of his spirit in your life. May you find comfort and joy in devoted friends. May he grant you his protection and peace. And overall, may you reflect the strength and love of God.

With joy you will draw water from the wells
of salvation.

Isaiah 12:3

The fruit of the Spirit is love, joy, peace,
patience, kindness, goodness,
faithfulness, gentleness and self control.

Galatians 5:22—23

Those who hope in the LORD will renew their
strength. They will soar on wings like
eagles; they will run and not grow weary,
they will walk and not be faint.

Isaiah 40:31

I pray that out of his glorious riches he may
strengthen you with power through his
Spirit in your inner being, so that Christ
may dwell in your hearts through faith.
And I pray that you, being rooted and established in love, may have power, together

with all the saints, to grasp how wide
and long and high and deep is the love of
Christ, and to know this love surpasses
knowledge—that you may be filled to the
measure of all the fullness of God.

Ephesians 3:16—19

You welcomed him with rich blessings, And
placed a crown of pure gold on his head.
He asked you for life, and you gave it to
him— Length of days, for ever and ever.

Psalm 21:3—4

No eye has seen, no ear has heard, no mind
has conceived what God has prepared for
those who love him.

1 Corinthians 2:9

The Lord is faithful, and he will strengthen
and protect you from the evil one.

2 Thessalonians 3:3

seek in prayerful words, dear friend, My heart's true wish to send you, That you may know that, far or near, My loving thoughts attend you. I cannot find a truer word, Nor better to address you; Nor song, nor poem have I heard Is sweeter than God bless you! God bless you! So I've wished you all of the brightness life possesses; For can there any joy at all Be yours unless God blesses? God bless you! So I breathe a charm Lest grief's dark night oppress you, For how can sorrow bring you harm If 'tis God's way to bless you?

Author unknown

Blessings on Your Wedding

Creating The Bouquet

*T*his wedding bouquet is not as difficult to make as it looks. Tuck white roses, white dendrodium orchids, white mini-carnations, and white stephanotis into a bouquet holder available from your florist or craft store. Tuck springs of ivy into the holder just under the flowers. If you prefer not to use a holder, gather the bouquet in your hand, criss-cross ribbon over the stems and tie it in a bow. Trim the stems even.

> **Supplies**
>
> • White Flower Holder with a Handle — these are available from florists or craft stores Some are edged with lace.

Meaning of Flowers

Dendrodium Orchid, *white*—**Refinement, nobility**

Stephanotis, *white*—**A wedding, happiness in marriage**

Rose, *white*—**Creative force, unity, joy**

Carnation, *white*—**Devoted love**

Ivy, *green*—**Wedded love, constancy, trustworthy**

Thoughtful additions if available

Verbena—faithfulness, fertility, marriage **Sweet Alyssum**—worth beyond beauty

Orange Blossom—your purity equals your loveliness, chastity, bridal festivities

Myrtle—married bliss, fidelity, love, home, peace, joy

Meaning of Bouquet

What a happy day! Joy and peace and love and delight be yours as God unites your hearts and lives!

You will go out in joy and be led forth in

    peace; the mountains and the hills will

burst forth into song before you, and all of

    the trees of the field will clap their

hands.

        Isaiah 55:12

How delightful is your love, my sister, my

    bride! How much more pleasing is your

love than wine, and the fragrance of your

    perfume than any spice! Your lips drop

sweetness as the honeycomb, my bride.

        Song of Songs 4:10—11

His mouth is sweetness itself; he is

    altogether lovely. This is my lover, this

my friend.

        Song of Songs 5:16

For this reason a man will leave his father

    and his mother and be united to his wife,

and the two will become one flesh.

        Ephesians 5:31

Your love, O Lord, reaches to the heavens,

    your faithfulness to the skies. They feast

on the abundance of your house; you give

    them drink from your river of delights.

For with you is the fountain of life; In your

    light we see light.

        Psalm 36:5,8—9

The bride belongs to the bridegroom. The

    friend who attends the bridegroom waits

and listens for him, and is full of joy when

    he hears the bridegroom's voice.

        John 3:29

Together I'm holding your hand like I said I would From the moment we knew this was blest and good. I'll be here beside you for better or worse. I promise to be with you, stay with you, love you forever. When the stormy skies have clouded up our eyes We will kneel before the throne and look for the light. And together we will love, together we will serve, together we will wait for the king.

Kathleen Le Pley

God Loves You

Creating the Bouquet

Hold two or three stems of white lilies lightly (they are easily wounded) in your hand. Surround with red Gerbera daisies. Add a few sprigs of Arborvitae (an evergreen shrub) and tie a wide satin bow around the stems. Trim the stems even.

Supplies
• Wide red satin ribbon

Meaning of Flowers

Lily, *white*—**Sweetness, purity, majesty**

Gerbera Daisy, *red*—**Loyal love**

Arborvitae, *evergreen*—**Unchanging devotion, tree of life**

Thoughtful additions if available

American Cowslip—Divine beauty, winning grace

Clematis, *pink, purple and white*—mental beauty, unchanged for eternity

Sweet Woodruff—Eternal life, rejoicing

Meaning of Bouquet

God, our majestic King, loves you with a loyal, everlasting love. In him are safety, satisfaction, light, and peace. Nothing can separate us from his unchanging love.

Jesus said, "Here I am! I stand at the door and knock. If anyone hears my voice and opens the door, I will come in and eat with him, and he with me."

Revelation 3:20

The LORD your God is with you, he is mighty to save. He will take great delight in you, he will quiet you with his love, he will rejoice over you with singing.

Zephaniah 3:17

Jesus declared, "I am the bread of life. He who comes to me will never go hungry, and he who believes in me will never be thirsty."

John 6:35

Jesus said, "I am the light of the world. Whoever follows me will never walk in darkness, but will have the light of life."

John 8:12

Whoever is wise, let him heed these things and consider the great love of the LORD.

Psalm 107:43

May the grace of the Lord Jesus Christ, and the love of God, and the fellowship of the Holy Spirit be with you all.

2 Corinthians 13:14

And I pray that you, being rooted and established in love, may have power, together with all the saints, to grasp how wide and long and high and deep is the love of Christ, and to know this love that surpasses knowledge—that you may be filled to the measure of all the fullness of God.

Ephesians 3:17—19

he love of God is greater far than tongue or pen can ever tell, It goes beyond the highest star and reaches to the lowest hell; The guilty pair, bowed down with care, God gave his Son to win; His erring child He reconciled and pardoned from his sin. O love of God, how rich and pure! How measureless and strong! It shall for evermore endure The saint's and angel's song. Could we with ink the ocean fill and were the skies of parchment made, Were every stalk on earth a quill and every man a scribe by trade, To write the love of God above would drain the ocean dry, Nor could the scroll contain the whole 'tho stretched from sky to sky.

Frederick M. Lehman

I Love You

Creating the Bouquet

$\mathcal{U}$se a glass vase of an interesting shape. Stuff lots of roses into the vase. Around and between them add cream-colored stock and rosy asters. Tuck in tulips of pink and rose-red to complete the bouquet. Tie the vase with a sheer ribbon.

Supplies

• Vase and Sheer Ribbon

Meaning of Flowers

Rose, *rose-red*—**Beauty, pride, love**

Tulip, *rose-red*—**Declarations of love**

Tulip, *pink*—**Love, imagination, dreams**

Asters, *deep pink*—**Sentimental memories**

Lemon Leaf, *green*—**Zest, fidelity, discretion**

Thoughtful additions if available

Sweet Marjoram—blushes, joy, mirth, kindness, courtesy

Forget-Me-Not—true love, hope, forget-me-not

Lilac—first emotions of love

Maidenhair Fern—discretion

Meaning of Bouquet

You are so beautiful to me. I love you!

Delight yourself in the Lord and he will give you the desires of your heart.

Psalm 37:4

Like a lily among thorns is my darling among the maidens.

Song of Songs 2:2

My lover is radiant and ruddy, outstanding among ten thousand.

Song of Songs 5:10

Above all, love each other deeply, because love covers over a multitude of sins.

1 Peter 4:8

Who is this that appears like the dawn, fair as the moon, bright as the sun, majestic as the stars in procession?

Song of Songs 6:10

And now these three remain: faith, hope and love. But the greatest of these is love.

1 Corinthians 13:13

There is no fear in love. But perfect love drives out fear, because fear has to do with punishment. The one who fears is not made perfect in love.

1 John 4:18

have never been rich before,
But you have poured Into my heart's
high door A golden hoard. My
wealth is the vision shared, The
sympathy, The feast of soul prepared
By you for me. Together we wander
through The wooded ways. Old
beauties are green and new Seen
through your gaze. I look for no
greater prize Than your soft voice.
The steadiness of your eyes Is my
heart's choice. I have never been rich
before, But I divine You step on my
sunlit floor And the wealth is mine!

Anne Campbell

Bless You on Your New Venture

Creating the Bouquet

Only three kinds of flowers make this stunning display suitable for a man or woman. Trim the stems of a dozen Dutch irises and put them in a glass vase. This one is an unusual oblong shape. Add yellow lily buds for the promise of good things to come. These will bloom out in a couple of days, making the bouquet even more beautiful. Add goldenrod (often called solidaster) to encourage the recipient on to greater things.

Supplies
- Glass vase

Meaning of Flowers

Buds, *any color*—**Promise of good things to come**
Dutch Iris, *blue, white, or yellow*—**My compliments, eloquence**
Goldenrod, *yellow*—**Encouragement**

Thoughtful additions if available

Pear—wise administration, benevolence
Coral Bells—hard work, challenge

Plum—courage, hardiness, perseverance, fidelity
Laurel—success, reward of merit

Meaning of Bouquet

This bouquet brings you wishes of great success and good things to come because of your new venture. As you commit your talent and your plan to God, may he gift you with boldness, endurance, and enthusiasm to reach your goal.

Be strong and courageous. Do not tremble or
be dismayed, for the LORD God is with
you wherever you go.
Joshua 1:9 (NAS)

In his heart a man plans his course, but the
LORD determines his steps.
Proverbs 16:9

When God gives any man wealth and pos-
sessions, and enables him to enjoy them,
to accept his lot and be happy with his
work—this is a gift of God.
Ecclesiastes 5:19

"I know the plans I have for you," declares
the LORD, "plans to prosper you and not
to harm you, plans to give you hope and a
future."
Jeremiah 29:11

May he give you the desire of your heart and
make all your plans succeed.
Psalm 20:4

Commit to the LORD whatever you do, and
your plans will succeed.
Proverbs 16:3

he mercy of God is an ocean divine,
A boundless and fathomless flood;
Launch out in the deep, cut away the
shoreline, And be lost in the fullness of
God. But many, alas! only stand on the
shore And gaze on the ocean so wide;
They never have ventured its depths to
explore, Or to launch from the fathomless
tide. And others just venture away from
the land, And linger so near to the shore,
That the surf and the slime that beat over
the strand, Dash o'er them in floods evermore. Oh, let us launch out on this ocean
so broad, Where the floods of salvation
e'er flow; Oh, let us be lost in the mercy
of God, Till the depths of his fullness we
know.

Albert B. Simpson, 1843—1919

Congratulations on Your New Baby

Creating the Bouquet

Use a baby bottle or a silver cup as a vase for this delightful little bouquet. Cut daisy stems to six-inches or less and put them into the container. Add pink carnations and blue delphinium. Stuff in little sprigs of baby's breath. You can add a white satin bow if you choose.

Supplies
• Baby bottle or Silver cup
• White satin for bow

Meaning of Flowers

English Daisy, *pink*—**New baby, innocence, simplicity, cheerfulness**
Delphinium, *blue*—**Sweetness**
Carnation, *pink*—**Maternal love, beauty, pride, pure affection**
Baby's Breath, *white*—**Pure heart, festivity**
Freesia, *many colors*—**Innocence**

Thoughtful additions if available
White Lilac—youthful innocence, purity, sweetness

Meaning of Bouquet

This bouquet represents the lovely beauty, innocence, and sweetness of your new baby. God has fulfilled the dream of giving you a precious child. May he now shower down protection, love, righteousness, and blessings on your child's life! Congratulations!

From everlasting to everlasting the LORD's
love is with those who fear him, and his
righteousness with their children's children.

Psalm 103:17

I praise you because I am fearfully and won-
derfully made; your works are wonderful, I know that full well.

Psalm 139:14

May your father and mother be glad; may
she who gave you birth rejoice!

Proverbs 23:25

I will pour water on the thirsty land, and
streams on the dry ground; I will pour
out my Spirit on your offspring, and my
blessing on your descendants.

Isaiah 44:3

Sons are a heritage from the LORD, children a
reward from him.

Psalm 127:3

Oh, that their hearts would be inclined to
fear me and keep all my commands
always, so that it might go well with them
and their children forever!

Deuteronomy 5:29

May your deeds be shown to your servants,
your splendor to their children.

Psalm 90:16

May the LORD make you increase, both you
and your children.

Psalm 115:14

A Child's Prayer

gracious Lord Jesus, creator of
all, I know that you love me,
although I'm so small. I do want to
praise you and follow your way,
Please forgive any way that I've hurt
you today. O thank you for fine
days, the bright stars, the sea! For
friends and dear family you've given
to me. Thank you for holding me
soft in your hand, And giving me
every new day from your plan. Help
me to see the whole world in your
light, And give me sweet peace
when I whisper, "Good night."

Marguerite Le Pley

Wishing You Good Health

Creating the Bouquet

*I*nsert a dozen roses in a tin canister. Choose pink roses or those that have some pink in them. Roses in this bouquet are pale yellow edged in pink. Tuck yarrow into the bouquet. White yarrow can often be found growing wild along roadways and in meadows. Domestic yarrow comes in white, yellow, and pink. Add galax leaves around the bottom of the bouquet. Tuck in sprigs of lemon balm.

> Supplies
>
> • Tin canister vase & Lemon balm plants — can be found at nurseries where herbs are sold.

Meaning of Flowers

Rose, *pink*—**Good health**

Yarrow, *white, yellow, pink*—**Health, healing of wounds, curing illness**

Galax, *green*—**Friendship, encouragement**

Lemon Balm, *green*—**Healing**

Thoughtful additions if available
Feverfew—warmth, good health

Meaning of Bouquet

This bouquet carries a prayer for your good health. May you put your trust in the Lord of strength; may your health be restored and may God give you perfect peace so that you sleep well. Get well soon!

Praise the LORD, O my soul; And forget not
all his benefits— Who forgives all your
sins and heals all your diseases.

Psalm 103:2—3

The LORD is my strength and my song; he
has become my salvation.

Exodus 15:2

I will lie down and sleep in peace, for you
alone, O LORD, make me dwell in safety.

Psalm 4:8

We wait in the hope for the LORD; he is our
help and our shield. In him our hearts
rejoice, for we trust in his holy name. May
your unfailing love rest upon us, O LORD,
even as we put our hope in you.

Psalm 33:20—22

A cheerful heart is good medicine.

Proverbs 17:22

Do not be wise in your own eyes; fear the
LORD and shun evil. This will bring
health to your body and nourishment to
your bones.

Proverbs 3:7—8

A cheerful look brings joy to the heart, and
good news gives health to the bones.

Proverbs 15:30

, Everlasting Light, giver of dawn and day, Dispeller of the ancient night in which creation lay! O, Everlasting Health, from which all healing springs, My bliss, my treasure, and my wealth, to thee my spirit clings. O, Everlasting Truth, truest of all that's true, Sure guide for erring age and youth, lead me and teach me too. O, Everlasting Strength, uphold me in the way; Bring me, in spite of foes, at length to joy and light and day. O Everlasting Love, wellspring of grace and peace, Pour down thy fullness from above, bid doubt and trouble cease.

Horatius Bonar, 1861

For My Friend

Creating the Bouquet

*H*ydrangeas are often given as potted plants, but they make excellent cut flowers as well. Cut blossoms and place them in a lovely vase. The flowers can later be hung upside down and dried for an everlasting bouquet.

Meaning of Flowers

Hydrangeas, *white, pink, blue*—**Devotion, remembrance**

Meaning of Bouquet

I am so thankful you are my friend. I remember all the wonderful times we've shared.

May God bless you today.

Dear friend, I pray that you may enjoy good
    health and that all may go well with you,
even as your soul is getting along well.

3 John 2

A cheerful look brings joy to the heart, and
    good news gives health to the bones.

Proverbs 15:30

Keep on loving each other.

Hebrews 13:1

Long life to you! Good health to you and
    your household! And good health to all
that is yours!

1 Samuel 25:6

I have not stopped giving thanks for you,
    remembering you in my prayers. I keep
asking that the God of our Lord Jesus Christ,
    the glorious Father, may give you the
Spirit of wisdom and revelation, so that you
    may know him better. I pray also that
the eyes of your heart may be enlightened in
    order that you may know the hope to
which he has called you, the riches of his
    glorious inheritance in the saints, and his
incomparably great power for us who
    believe.

Ephesians 5:16—19

I shot an arrow into the air,
It fell to earth, I knew not where;
For, so swiftly it flew, the sight
Could not follow in its flight.
I breathed a song into the air,
It fell to earth, I knew not where;
For who has sight so keen and strong
That it can follow the flight of song?
Long, long afterward, in an oak
I found the arrow, still unbroke;
And the song, from beginning to end,
I found again in the heart of a friend.

Henry Wadsworth Longfellow

God Be with You

Creating the Bouquet

Find the freshest, most beautiful zinnias available. Choose any combination of favorite colors. Gather twelve to fifteen of them in your hand and tuck in sprigs of arborvitae. Tie it all with a matching narrow satin ribbon.

Supplies
• Narrow satin ribbon to match bouquet

Meaning of Flowers

Zinnia, *many colors***—Thoughts of absent friends**
Arborvitae, *green***—Unchanging devotion**

Meaning of Bouquet

No matter where you go or what you do, may God hold you close. May he guide you and keep you throughout your life. Remember that we love you and are devoted to you. Our thoughts are ever with you.

The LORD bless you and keep you; The LORD make his face shine upon you and be gracious to you; The LORD turn his face toward you and give you peace.

Numbers 6:24—26

If you make the Most High your dwelling— even the LORD who is my refuge —then no harm will befall you, no disaster will come near your tent. For he will command his angels concerning you to guard you in all your ways; they will lift you up in their hands, so that you will not strike your foot against a stone.

Psalm 91:9—12

If I rise on the wings of the dawn, if I settle at the far side of the sea, even there your hand will guide me, your right hand will hold me fast.

Psalm 139:9,10

Come, let us bow down in worship, let us kneel before the LORD our Maker; for he is our God and we are the people of his pasture, the flock under his care.

Psalm 95:6—7

But let all who take refuge in you be glad; let them ever sing for joy. Spread your protection over them, that those who love your name may rejoice in you. For surely, O LORD, you bless the righteous; you surround them with your favor as with a shield.

Psalm 5:11—12

Cast your cares on the LORD and he will sustain you; he will never let the righteous fall.

Psalm 55:22

Keep me safe, O God, for in you I take refuge.

Psalm 16:1

The LORD will watch over your coming and going both now and forevermore.

Psalm 121:8

God Be With You

ay his counsels sweet
  uphold you,
And his loving arms enfold you,
As you journey on your way.
May his sheltering wings protect you,
And his light divine direct you,
Turning darkness into day.
May his potent peace surround you,
 And his presence linger with you,
As your inner, golden ray.

Author unknown

Congratulations on Your Performance

Creating the Bouquet

Lay one to two dozen coral-colored roses on a sheet of iridescent cellophane in a cascading fashion. Insert dutch iris and bouvardia throughout the bouquet. Add short branches and springs of boxwood. Wrap the cellophane around the bouquet and tie it with a sheer coral-colored ribbon.

Supplies

• Cellophane — available from your florist or craft store.

• Sheer Ribbon

Meaning of Flowers

Bouvardia, *pink, white*—**Enthusiasm**

Rose, *coral*—**I admire your accomplishments**

Dutch Iris, *blue, yellow or white*—**My compliments, eloquence**

Boxwood, *green*—**Hard work**

Thoughtful additions if available

Coral Bells—hard work

Coneflower/Echinachea—skill, capability

Fuchsia—good taste

Laurel—success, reward of merit

Meaning of Bouquet

My compliments for your wonderful performance! I admire your accomplishments. Your success is the reward of your enthusiastic, diligent work—God has blessed you—Congratulations!

Come and see what God has done, how
awesome his works in man's behalf!
Psalm 66:5

The sluggard craves and gets nothing, but
the desires of the diligent are fully
satisfied.
Proverbs 13:4

Trust in the LORD with all your heart and
lean not on your own understanding; in
all your ways acknowledge him, and he will
make your paths straight
Proverbs 3:5—6

How great is your goodness, which you have
stored up for those who fear you, which
you bestow in the sight of men on those
who take refuge in you.
Psalm 31:19

The LORD is my strength and my shield; my
heart trusts in him, and I am helped. My
heart leaps for joy and I will give thanks to
him in song.
Psalm 28:7

But eagerly desire the greater gifts. And now
I will show you the most excellent way.
1 Corinthians 12:31

Whatever is true, whatever is noble, whatever is right, whatever is pure, whatever
is lovely, whatever is admirable—if anything
is excellent or praiseworthy—think about
such things. Whatever you have learned or
received or heard from me, or seen in
me—put it into practice. And the God of
peace will be with you.
Philippians 4:8—9

For the LORD your God will bless you in all
your harvest and in all the work of your
hands, and your joy will be complete.
Deuteronomy 16:15

Chisel in hand stood a sculptor boy

With his marble block before him,

And his eyes lit up with a smile of joy,

As an angel dream passed o'er him.

He carved the dream on that shapeless stone,

With many a sharp incision;

With heaven's own light the sculpture
shone—

He'd caught that angel vision.

Children of life are we, as we stand

With our lives uncarved before us,

Waiting the hour when, at God's command,

Our life dream shall pass o'er us.

If we carve it then on yielding stone,

With many a sharp incision,

Its heavenly beauty shall be our own—

Our lives, that angel vision.

George Washington Doane, 1700—1859

I am Praying for You

Creating the Bouquet

Purchase a nice basket with a handle and a plastic liner. Tuck in small geranium plants. This bouquet has five small red geranium plants and one with variegated leaves for contrast. (Spring, summer, fall.)

Supplies
• Basket — available from florist or craft store.
• Geraniums — available at a nursery.

Meaning of Flowers

Geranium, *red*—**Comfort, health, protection**

Thoughtful additions if available
Lemon Balm Leaf—healing, sympathy, drives away heaviness of mind
Pine—warmth, friendship, vigor, endurance, spiritual energy
Thrift/armeria—sympathy
Thyme—bravery, courage, strength

Meaning of Bouquet

I am praying that you will see the Lord before you—greater than any foe; that you will take refuge in him and he will uphold you with his mighty right hand, and turn your darkness into light. I'm wishing you good health, comfort, and protection.

The eternal God is your refuge, and under-

neath are the everlasting arms.

Deuteronomy 33:27

I have set the LORD always before me.

Because he is at my right hand, I will

not be shaken.

Psalm 16:8

The LORD is my light and my salvation—

whom shall I fear? The LORD is the

stronghold of my life— of whom shall I

be afraid?

Psalm 27:1

Dear friend, I pray that you may enjoy good

health and that all may go well with you.

3 John 2

I love the LORD, for he heard my voice; he

heard my cry for mercy. Because he

turned his ear to me, I will call on him as

long as I live. The cords of death entan-

gled me, the anguish of the grave came upon

me; I was overcome by trouble and sor-

row. Then I called on the name of the LORD:

"O LORD, save me!" The LORD is gracious

and righteous; our God is full of compassion.

The LORD protects the simplehearted;

when I was in great need, he saved me. Be at

rest once more, O my soul, for the LORD

has been good to you. For you, O LORD, have

delivered my soul from death, my eyes

from tears, my feet from stumbling, that I

may walk before the LORD in the land of

the living.

Psalm 116:1—9

Quietly I enter the closet Quietly I close the door. Outside are the futilities, The doubts and useless struggles; Forgotten are the little things That too long have shackled my mind And held me prisoner. Now unhurried and free I contemplate God, His mercy and His love. Patiently I wait. Lo, out of the shadows Comes His presence. Silently we visit. From His wounded hand I receive His balm And His comfort. I rest. The door to the world is opened! Eagerly I pass, No longer futile, Nor fearful, Nor yet alone. No longer I, But, We!

P.M. Snider

Flowers Used in This Book

Alstroemeria—devotion, friendship, pleasantries

Angelica Leaf—inspirations, soaring thoughts

Aster—sentimental memories

Baby's breath—pure heart, festivity

Blue Salvia—wisdom, I think of you

Bouvardia—enthusiasm

Boxwood—hard work

Buds—promise of good things to come

Calla Lily—magnificent beauty, feminine modesty

Carnation, *white*—devoted love

Carnation, *pink*—maternal love, beauty, pride, pure affection

Chrysanthemum—optimism, cheerfulness, joy, mirth

Clematis—mental beauty, ingenuity

Coneflower/ echinachea—skill, capability

Coral Bells—hard work

Daffodil—regard, respect

Daisy Fleabane—thank you

Delphinium—well being, sweetness, return of a friend is desired

Dendrodium Orchid—love, beauty, refinement

Dutch Iris—my compliments, eloquence

English Daisy—new baby, innocence, simplicity

Evergreen—longevity

Fern—fascination, sincerity

Feverfew—warmth, good health

Forget-me-not—true love, hope, forget me not

Freesia—innocence

Fuchsia—good taste

Galax leaves—friendship, encouragement

Gerbera daisy—beauty

Gladiolus—strength of character, generosity

Globe Amaranth—purpose, immortality, eternal love

Goldenrod—encouragement

Heather—admiration, dreams accomplished

Honeysuckle—bonds of love, generous and devoted affection

Ivy—wedded love, constancy, trustfulness, fidelity

Larkspur—open-hearted

Laurel—success, reward of merit

Lavender—devotion, success, tranquility

Leather Fern—sincerity, fascination

Lemon Balm Leaf—healing, sympathy, drives away heaviness of mind

Lemon Leaf—zest, fidelity, discretion

Lilac, *purple*—first emotions of love

Lilac, *white*—youthful innocence, purity, sweetness

Lily of the Valley—sweetness, return of happiness, purity, delicacy

Lily—majesty, resurrection

Magnolia Leaf—perseverance, sweetness, beauty

Maidenhair Fern—discretion

Mini Carnation Buds—promise of good things to come, pure affection

Mint—welcome, hospitality, warmth of feelings, wisdom

Morning Glory—the evanescent loveliness of life

Myrtle—married bliss, fidelity, love, home, peace, joy

Oak—hospitality

Orange Blossom—your purity equals your loveliness, chastity, bridal festivities

Pansy—loving thoughts, you occupy my thoughts

Pear—wise administration, benevolence

Phlox—our souls are united, proposal of love, sweet dreams

Pine—warmth, friendship, vigor, endurance, spiritual energy

Pink asters—sentimental recollections

Plum—courage, hardiness, perseverance, fidelity

Queen Anne's Lace—protection, haven, comfort, home, I'll return

Red geranium—comfort, health, protection

Rosemary—remembrance, fidelity, devotion, your presence revives me, wisdom, strong memory

Roses, *coral*—I admire your accomplishments
    gold—absolute achievement
    lavender—rarity, dignity
    peach—let's get together
    pink—good health
    red—I love you, desire, passion, harmony, joy, charm, beauty
    rose-red—beauty, pride, love
    white—creative force, unity, joy

Sage—domestic virtue

Salad Burnet—a merry heart, joy

Sea Statice—remembrance

Sorrel—joy, parental affection

Statice—remembrance, gratitude

Stephanotis—happiness in marriage

Stock—promptness, lasting beauty

Sweet Alyssum—worth beyond beauty

Sweet Marjoram—blushes, joy, mirth, kindness, courtesy

Sweet Woodruff—eternal life, rejoicing

Thrift/Armeria—sympathy

Thyme—bravery, courage, strength

Tulip, *many colors*—the perfect lover, happy years, memory, charity
    pink—love, imagination, dreams
    rose-red—declarations of love

Verbena—faithfulness, fertility, marriage

Viola/Johnny Jump-up—happy thoughts

White Chrysanthemum—truth

White pinks—ingenuity, talent

Yarrow—health, healing of wounds, curing illness

Zinnia—thoughts of absent friends

Sources

Peggy Benson, et al. Friends Through Thick and Thin (Grand Rapids, MI: Zondervan Publishing House, 1998).

Anne Campbell, "To My Friend," Copyright (c) 1947 by Anne Campbell.

Kathleen Le Pley, "Together," Lyrics used by permission of the author.

Rice, Helen Steiner, "A Mother's Love," Gifts of Love (Grand Rapids, MI: Fleming H. Revell, 1993).

Rosa Marinoni Zagnoni, "For the New Home."